Spiders

Donna Bailey

Steck-Vaughn
LIBRARY
A Division of Steck-Vaughn Company

Have you ever found a spider's web
in your yard?
The dew on this web makes it shine in
the early morning sunlight.
The spider that made the web is waiting
nearby to catch its prey.

2

A spider has eight long legs and
its body is divided into two parts.
Can you see a pattern of whitish spots
on the back of this garden spider?
The spots make the shape of a cross.

The spider's eyes, mouth, and jaws
are on the front half of its body.
The sharp fangs in a spider's jaw
have poison in them for killing prey.
Next to the jaws are the pedipalps.
Most spiders use pedipalps to cut
and crush their food.

Underneath its body the spider has
six little spinnerets that it uses
to spin silk for its web.
Before it spins silk, the spider makes a liquid
inside its body.
The liquid comes out of the spinnerets
as a strong, elastic silk.

Garden spiders spin large, wheel-like webs
called orbs.
They use their webs to trap insects.
The spider usually spins a new web
every morning, just before dawn.
It takes about 20 minutes to spin a web.

The spider first spins a single thread
called the bridge line.
The bridge line is carried by the wind until
it catches on a twig or a leaf.
The spider then makes the outer frame
of the web.

When the frame is finished, the spider
spins the radial threads.
These go from the center of the web to
the outside, like the spokes in a wheel.
Then, working from the center, the spider
lays down a non-sticky spiral.
The spiral holds the radial threads together.

Now the spider works back toward the center,
spinning a spiral of sticky threads.
It eats the non-sticky spiral as it goes.
Finally the spider makes a platform
at the center of the web.
The spider sits there to wait for its prey.

At sunrise, the spider leaves the web
and hides under a nearby leaf.
The spider puts a claw on a thread
that is connected to the web.
When an insect is trapped,
the web begins to shake.

The spider rushes to the middle
of the web and bites its prey.
Poison from its fangs kills the insect.
The spider wraps the insect in
silk threads and carries it to a safe place.

Spiders have very small mouths and cannot swallow solid food.
The juices from the spider's fangs make the soft parts of the prey turn liquid.
The spider sucks up the liquid and throws away the hard outer shell of the insect.

Male spiders are usually smaller than females.
When a male spider wants to mate with
a female spider, he must be very careful.
The male drums on the female's web
to tell her he is coming.
After mating, the male tries to escape
before the female can eat him!

In autumn, garden spiders lay their eggs
in golden-yellow cocoons made of silk.
Each cocoon contains 600 to 800 eggs.
The female spider fastens the cocoon
to a safe place.

The eggs hatch the following June and
the spiderlings cluster together.
A mass of tiny strands of silk holds the
spiderlings together in a ball.

After a few days, the spiderlings scatter.
Each spiderling spins a long thread.
The thread is caught by the wind.
Each spiderling is carried to a new spot
where it can spin its own small web.

The spiderlings reach their full size
the following summer.
Then the female spiders spin huge orb webs
and get ready to mate.
Most adult spiders don't live through winter.
They usually die in the late fall.

Not all spiders spin webs to catch their prey.
Some hunting spiders catch their prey
by speed and cunning.
This wolf spider digs a small burrow
in soft dirt.
It shelters inside its burrow during the day.

18

The wolf spider leaves the burrow
at night to catch small insects.
The spider runs after insects and grabs them
in its strong jaws.
This Australian wolf spider has found
some termites to eat.

Wolf spiders can move fast and
need good eyesight to see their prey.
They have four small eyes in the lowest row,
two very large eyes in the middle row, and
two medium-sized eyes in the top row.

20

Crab spiders use camouflage
to help them catch their prey.
They hide in flowers that match
the color of their body.
The butterfly visiting this flower
did not see the spider hiding inside it.

Crab spiders are usually quite small.
When they move, they scuttle sideways
like crabs on the seashore.
That is why they are called crab spiders.
This crab spider is on an oak leaf.

Some of the biggest spiders in the world
are the bird-eating spiders that live
in South America.
The hairy body of a bird-eating spider
can be up to four inches long.
Its leg span can be 10 inches across.

During the day, a bird-eating spider hides
in the crack of a rock or in the hole of a tree.
At night the spider runs after prey and
grabs it in a sudden, silent dash.
It often catches small birds.
This spider has caught a large grasshopper.

Trap-door spiders dig holes in the ground.

The hole may be as much as

one foot deep and two inches across.

The spider lines its hole with silk.

The spider makes a round lid of silk and soil to close the mouth of the hole. The lid is hinged so that when the spider climbs into its hole, it can pull the lid shut behind it.

When it wants to catch some food,
the trap-door spider lifts the lid
and looks out.
If an insect is nearby, the spider
rushes out to pounce on its prey.

This trap-door spider has caught and
killed a beetle.
It drags its victim back to its hole,
pulls it inside, and closes the lid after it.

Water spiders make their home underwater
in ponds and streams.
The spider needs air to breathe, so
it makes a diving bell.
The diving bell traps and stores air.

The water spider first spins a platform of silk between the stems and leaves of water plants.
Then it goes to the surface of the pond.
The spider uses its legs to trap a bubble of air under its body.

The spider swims down to the platform, or
climbs down the stem of a plant.
It puts the bubble of air under the platform.
The spider does the same thing again and
again until the web takes on a bell shape.

The spider stays inside the bell during
the day, and waits for a small fish or
insect to swim by.

The spider then grabs the fish and
takes it to its bell to eat it.

Index

Editorial Consultant: Donna Bailey
Executive Editor: Elizabeth Strauss
Project Editor: Becky Ward

Picture research by Jennifer Garratt
Designed by Richard Garratt Design

Photographs
Cover: Bruce Coleman (Jane Burton)
Bruce Coleman: title page, 5 (P.A. Hinchcliffe); 2, 31 (Adrian Davies); 3 (G. Dore); 10 (John Markham);
12 (Andy Purcell); 15, 16, 21, 22, 29, 30 (Jane Burton); 20, 23 (Hans Reinhard); 25, 26 (Jan Taylor)
OSF Picture Library: 4, 7, 8, 9, 14, 17, 32 (J.A.L. Cooke); 6 (Michael Leach); 11 (Raymond Blythe);
13 (M.F. Black); 18 (P. & W. Ward); 19 (Mantis Wildlife Films); 24 (Partridge Productions); 27, 28 (Sean Morris)

Library of Congress Cataloging-in-Publication Data: Bailey, Donna. Spiders / Donna Bailey. p. cm.—
(Animal world) Includes index. SUMMARY: Studies the physical characteristics, behavior, and life cycles of different
kinds of spiders. ISBN 0-8114-2648-3 1. Spiders—Juvenile literature. [1. Spiders.] I. Title. II. Series: Animal
world (Austin, Tex.) QL452.2.B35 1991 595.4′4—dc20 90-22113 CIP AC